One Smart Fish

Written by Laura Manivong
Illustrated by Suzanne Beaky

Children's Press®
A Division of Scholastic Inc.
New York • Toronto • London • Auckland • Sydney
Mexico City • New Delhi • Hong Kong
Danbury, Connecticut

For Troy, Clara & Aidan…my very own school of smart fish
—L.M.

To my Mom and Dad, who were always there for me
—S.B.

Reading Consultant

Eileen Robinson
Reading Specialist

Library of Congress Cataloging-in-Publication Data

Manivong, Laura, 1967-
  One smart fish / written by Laura Manivong ; illustrated by Suzanne Beaky.
      p. cm. — (A rookie reader)
  Summary: A child tries to catch a fish using such bait as hot dog meat, cookie dough, and spaghetti.
  ISBN 0-516-24982-7 (lib. bdg.)   0-516-24996-7 (pbk.)
  [1. Fishing—Fiction. 2. Stories in rhyme.] I. Beaky, Suzanne, 1971- ill. II. Title. III. Series.
  PZ8.3.M353On 2006
  [E]—dc22
                                    2005016132

I want to catch a fish to eat.

I bait my hook with hot dog meat.

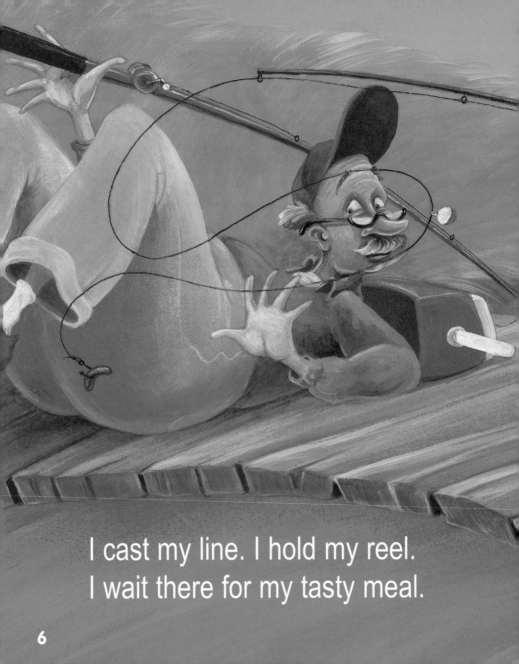

I cast my line. I hold my reel.
I wait there for my tasty meal.

I get no bites. I check my hook.
The hot dog's gone.

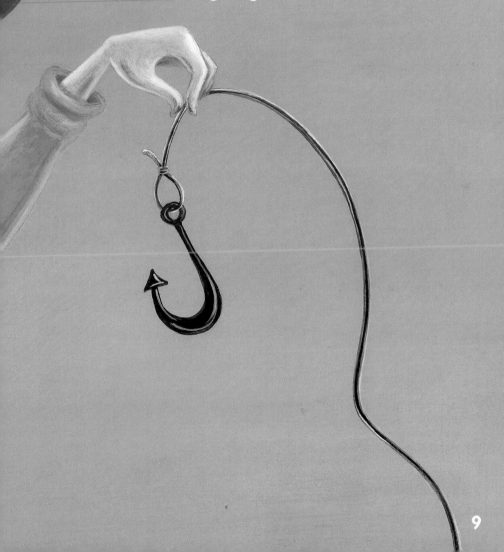

"Hey, fish! You crook!"

The wind picks up.
Clouds roll in.

I hear a plop. I spy a fin.

It starts to rain
but I won't go.
I bait my line
with cookie dough.

I feel a twitch.
I check once more.

18

He stole again, just like before!

I have a trick. That fish won't win.

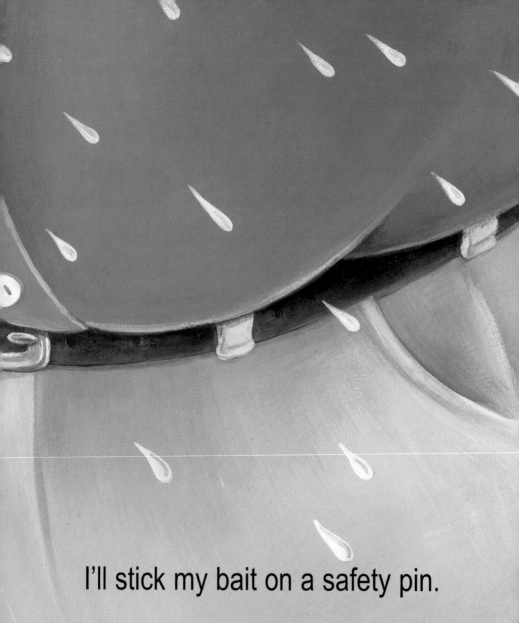

I'll stick my bait on a safety pin.

I hook on Grandpa's prized spaghetti.

I'm robbed again! I quit already!

That fish is smarter than I knew.
What'd I catch? A cold! ACHOO!

Word List (84 Words)

(Words in **bold** are story words that rhyme.)

a	**dough**	I	picks	than
achoo	**eat**	I'll	**pin**	that
again	feel	I'm	plop	the
already	**fin**	**in**	prized	there
bait	fish	is	quit	to
before	for	it	rain	trick
bites	get	just	**reel**	twitch
but	**go**	**knew**	robbed	up
cast	gone	like	roll	wait
catch	grandpa's	line	safety	want
check	have	**meal**	smarter	what'd
clouds	he	**meat**	**spaghetti**	**win**
cold	hear	**more**	spy	wind
cookie	hey	my	starts	with
crook	hold	no	stick	won't
dog	**hook**	on	stole	you
dog's	hot	once	tasty	

About the Author

Laura Manivong lives in Kansas City, Kansas, with her husband, two kids, two dogs, and an albino squirrel in the backyard. She works at a television station making commercials. She likes to take her dogs to the lake so they can fish. All they catch are tennis balls and sticks.

About the Illustrator

Suzanne Beaky grew up in Columbus, Ohio, where she studied illustration at Columbus College of Art and Design. She now lives in Kirksville, Missouri, with her husband and four cats. She has never caught a fish either.